Other books by Brian...

...the Staffroom Door

...est of Brian Moses

...d Elvis

...rian Moses

...as

...that

...n likes to

think that maybe ... ong.

Contact Brian via his website:
www.brianmoses.co.uk, and check out his blog:
brian-moses.blogspot.com

David Parkins does his best, but it's not good enough. Instead of working hard, David seems to waste all his time drawing pictures. He has shown some promise in this, doing illustrations for books, comics, newspapers and magazines, but although his drawings are brilliant and funny he is rarely on time. David moved to Canada with his family in 2006. He has five cats, but only four chairs in his studio, so he usually works standing up. This can be uncomfortable, and may be why he is always ... ays he is very ...

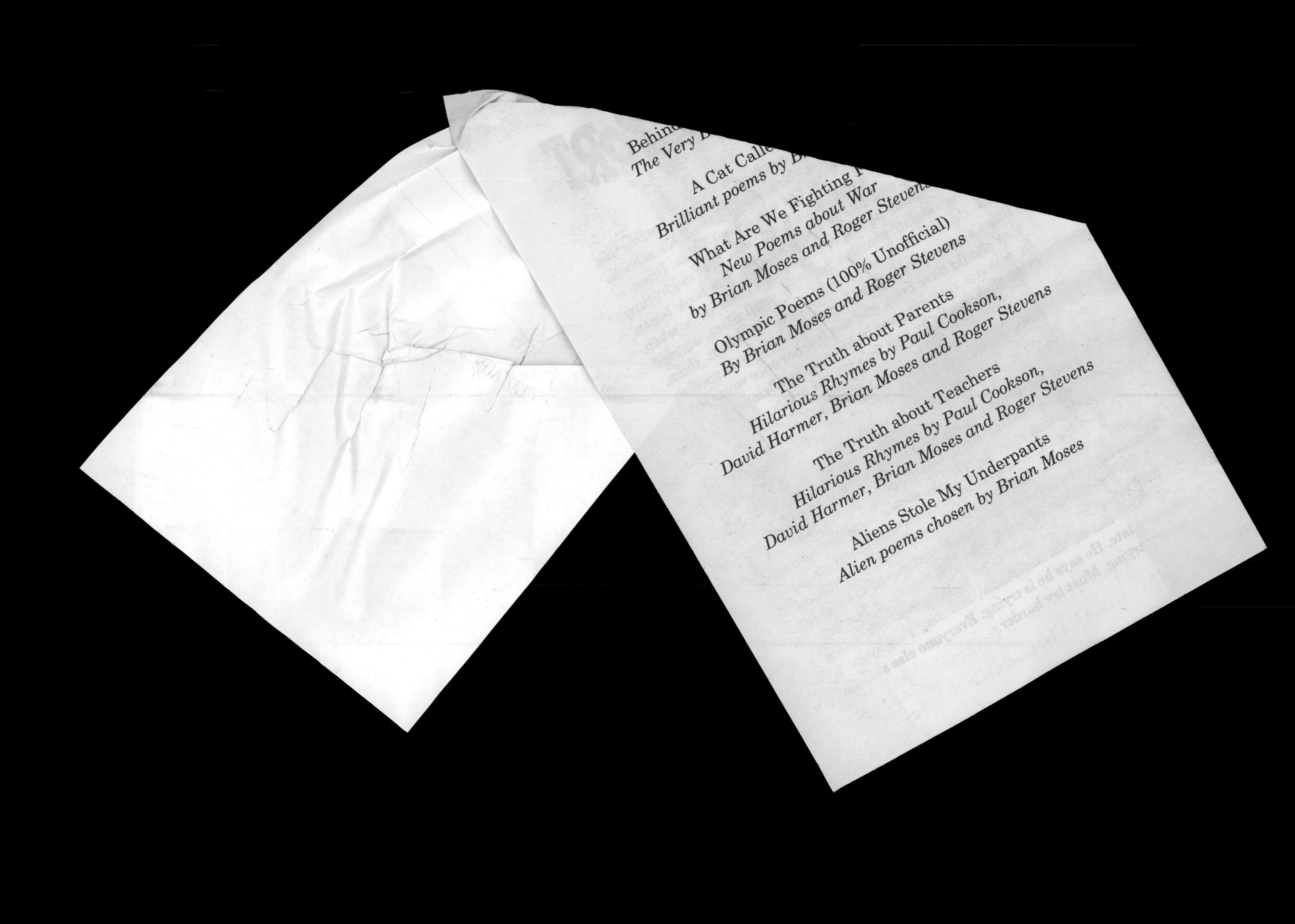
Behind
The Very B

A Cat Calle
Brilliant poems by B

What Are We Fighting F
New Poems about War
by Brian Moses and Roger Stevens

Olympic Poems (100% Unofficial)
By Brian Moses and Roger Stevens

The Truth about Parents
Hilarious Rhymes by Paul Cookson,
David Harmer, Brian Moses and Roger Stevens

The Truth about Teachers
Hilarious Rhymes by Paul Cookson,
David Harmer, Brian Moses and Roger Stevens

Aliens Stole My Underpants
Alien poems chosen by Brian Moses

Illustrated by David Parkins

MACMILLAN CHILDREN'S BOOKS

First published 2014 by Macmillan Children's Books
a division of Macmillan Publishers Limited
20 New Wharf Road, London N1 9RR
Basingstoke and Oxford
Associated companies throughout the world
www.panmacmillan.com

ISBN 978-1-4472-5464-5

1 3 5 7 9 8 6 4 2

A CIP catalogue record for this book is available from the British Library.

Printed and bound by CPI Group (UK) Ltd, Croydon CR0 4YY

For children and teachers in schools on Jersey and Guernsey where I have worked on many occasions

Contents

Targets

My teacher says my targets are:

To write more neatly,
to spell more words correctly,
to get more sums right,
to chatter less
and to behave myself.

But the targets I set myself
are far more interesting:

To climb a tree to the top,
to stop time before my spelling test,
to think up a disappearing spell
and try it out on my teacher,
to leap from up high
and to defy gravity.

These are my targets,
the ones I'm aiming to complete
before next week . . .

The ones my teacher sets
may take a little longer . . .

Classroom Groups

In class one the bees are buzzing all day
but snowy owls just sit and stare.
The hippos get in everyone's way
while antelopes run everywhere.

In class two blue group look quite blue
and yellow group never look well.
Red group blush quite easily
but black group are sheer hell!

Tens, units, fractions, decimals,
class three groups are mathematical.
Pronouns, adjectives, verbs and nouns,
in class four everyone's grammatical.

In class five it's the great composers,
Mozart, Vivaldi, Beethoven and Bach.
Beethoven don't hear much at all
but Mozart sing sweet as a lark.

This term class six are geographical,
mountains, valleys, rivers and streams,
but last term's topic 'food' was brill
with chocolate, pizza, chips, ice creams.

I wonder if teachers have their groups too
when they're snacking in the staffroom and
we can't see?
The Pot Noodle lunchers, banana munchers,
the ones who drink coffee and never touch tea.

In our school there's lots of different groups
but I like to make up more of my own.
There are groups good at maths or drawing or
games
and mine who are good at going home!

Behind the Staffroom Door

Ten tired teachers slumped in the staffroom
at playtime,
one collapsed when the coffee ran out, then
there were nine.

Nine tired teachers making lists of things
they hate,
one remembered playground duty, then there
were eight.

Eight tired teachers thinking of holidays in
Devon,
one slipped off to pack his case, then there
were seven.

Seven tired teachers, weary of children's
tricks,
one hid in the stock cupboard, then there were
six.

Six tired teachers, under the weather, barely
alive,
one gave an enormous sneeze, then there were
five.

Five tired teachers, gazing at the open door,
one made a quick getaway, then there were
four.

Four tired teachers, faces lined with misery,
one locked herself in the ladies, then there
were three.

Three tired teachers, wondering what to do,
one started screaming when the bell rang,
then there were two.

Two tired teachers, thinking life really ought
to be fun,
one was summoned to see the head, then
there was one.

One tired teacher caught napping in the
afternoon sun,
fled quickly from the staffroom, then there
were none.

Middle Names

Do you know your teacher's middle name?

Would it be one that they'd be
too embarrassed to reveal?

Maybe it's something potty like Dotty
or silly like Chantilly,
something divine like Columbine
or medicinal like Calamine,
something modern like Ikea
or historical like Boadicea.

Perhaps it's something seasonal
like Primrose,
or a name that gets up your nose
like Hyacinth.

Maybe it's American like Hank
or solid and British like Frank.
Maybe it's barbaric like Conan
or boy-bandish and poppy
like Ronan.

Perhaps it's old-fashioned
like Dora and Norah,
or something buttery
like Flora.

Maybe it's expensive like Pearl
or with a country twang like Merle.
Is it something classy like Clancy
or fancy like Nancy,
something Biblical like Zachariah,
Amos, Moses or Jeremiah?

Is it witchy like Winnie
or moany like Minnie,
sensible like Fred,
countrified like Ned?

Is it tragic like Romeo
or Italian like Antonio?

Is it Zebedee or Gertrude,
Marvin or Ermintrude?
Is it Cecil or Boris,
Marmaduke or Doris?

Now go spread rumours
all around school.
Your teachers have names
that just aren't cool.

It's sure to embarrass them!

Cakes in the Staffroom

Nothing gets teachers more excited
than cakes in the staffroom at break-time.
Nothing gets them more delighted
than the sight of plates
piled high with jammy doughnuts
or chocolate cake.

It's an absolute stampede
as the word gets round quickly.

And it's, 'Oooh, these are really delicious,'
and, 'Aaah, these doughnuts are great.'

And you hear them say, 'I really shouldn't,'
or, 'Just a tiny bit, I'm on a diet.'

Really, it's the only time they're quiet
when they're cramming cakes into their
mouths,
when they're wearing a creamy moustache
or the jam squirts out like blood,
or they're licking chocolate
from their fingers.

You can tell when they've been scoffing,
they get lazy in literacy,
sleepy in silent reading,
nonsensical in numeracy,
look guilty in assembly.

But nothing gets teachers more excited
than cakes in the staffroom at break-time,
unless of course,
it's wine in the staffroom at lunchtime!

Day Closure

We had a day closure on Monday
and I spent the morning in bed,
but the teachers went in as usual
and someone taught them instead.

And I thought of them all in the classroom,
stuck to their seats in rows,
some of them sucking pen lids,
head teacher scratching his nose.

Perhaps it's a bit like an MOT
to check if teachers still know
the dates of our kings and queens
or the capital of so-and-so.

Perhaps they had tables and spellings,
did the head give them marks out of ten?
And then, if they got any wrong,
did he make them learn them again?

I thought of them out at break-time
playing football or kiss-chase or tag,
picking up teams in the playground
or scoffing crisps from a bag.

If I'd been a fly on the wall,
I might have watched while they slaved,
I'd have seen who asked silly questions
or if anyone misbehaved.

I thought of them all going home,
crossing the road to their mums.
They looked very grim the next day.
It couldn't have been much fun.

I'd Rather Be Doing Anything Today Than . . .

I'd rather be doing anything today
than going to school.

I'd rather tightrope-walk across the Grand
Canyon
or tumble over Niagara Falls in a barrel.

I'd rather have my feet nibbled by piranhas
or try to tiptoe past a sleepy lion.

I'd rather eat Brussels sprouts for my birthday
tea
or bungee-jump from the Empire State Building.

I'd rather wander through the town in my
underwear
or practise juggling with dynamite.

I'd rather kiss a pot-bellied pig
or sleep in a nest of vipers.

I'd rather walk through a haunted forest at
night
or be invited to tea at Dracula's Castle.

I'd rather have a spitting contest with a camel or be forced to eat sardine sandwiches.

Yes, I'd rather be doing anything today than going to school . . .

Because school's just not cool enough for me.

(I'm sure you can add other ideas to this yourself . . .)

How Teachers Leave School Each Evening

The dance teacher floats down the stairway
and waltzes herself to the door.
Behind her the maths teacher counts every step
as he paces across the floor.

The geography teacher struggles to find
a different route home each night.
The PE teacher sets new daily records
for the swiftest homeward flight.

The English teacher recites to himself
lines of poetry by Keats.
The drama teacher's on camera,
a movie star in the streets.

The RE teacher prays
that there'll be no traffic queues.
The physics teacher knows there will
and regularly blows a fuse.

The IT teacher imagines he's left
as he follows some virtual route on screen.
It's a mystery why the history teacher
is met each night by a limousine.

Our music teacher, an Elvis freak,
plays air guitar along the drive.
With his rocker's quiff and Las Vegas suit
he's out there somewhere perfecting his jive.

But the teacher who's young and still keen
reluctantly closes the door,
ticks off the hours and minutes till she can be
back with her class once more.

Dragon Path

(For Crowhurst village school, who gave this name to a path in their playground)

Nothing will be the same as before
once you've drawn a dragon to your door,
once a dragon knows just where to find you
you'll always have to look behind you,
always have to take great care
once you summon a dragon from its lair.
And it won't be any kind of joke
if you see flames, if you smell smoke
or wake to find in dread of night,
half the village set alight.
Then next day finding your head teacher
protecting the school from this fearful creature,
flameproofing the roof, soundproofing the doors
to block out the noise of its dragony roars.
While you're inside, preparing for SATS,
the dragon is feasting on barbecued cats.
Avoiding the dragon will drive you insane.
I suggest you rename your path 'Sweet Hamster
  Lane'.

Classroom Globe

We strung our globe from the rafters
then watched as the continents spun.
We were dizzy with faraway places,
they swam before our eyes.
Everyone wanted to take a swipe at
the planet, to roll the world, to cause
global chaos. We laughed at the
notion of some great hand, sweeping down
avalanches, rolling earthquakes round
Africa, knocking elephants off their feet.
Then reasons were found for leaving seats,
to touch or tilt or hit heads on the planet,
squaring up to the world like March hares.
We talked of how the earth had been
    damaged,
leaving it bruised, sore from neglect,
and Jenny, who feels sorry for anyone and
anything, leaned her brow against the planet
and felt the sorrow and pain of earth
in a cold hard globe.

Astronaut School

Wouldn't it be cool to go to Astronaut School,
to unravel the mysteries of space travel,
to find out what the universe is all about,
from the mathematics of rocket ships
to the science of a lunar eclipse?
Wouldn't it be brill to fill your head
with formulas for the right type of rocket fuel,
or for working out how much thrust
you must have to land safely on Mars?
Wouldn't it be great to practise
moonwalking in games, and instead of French
learn Martian or Venusian
knowing that someday, when your training was
  done,
you might even go where they're spoken?
Wouldn't it be fab to learn about lunar habitats,
to discover what grows in dust
or what stops rust on satellites?

All in all it's clever stuff,
far too clever for me.
I'll just stay here and dream my way
through English, maths and PE.

Lost-Property Box

In our lost-property box
there are socks with holes in
and shoes minus laces,
stand-up figures
without any bases,
a faded T-shirt
from Lanzarote,
a greatest-hits tape
by Pavarotti,
once-champion conkers
shrunken with age,
a mystery book
without the last page,
sandwich boxes
with last month's bread in,
PE shorts
I wouldn't be seen dead in,
unloved toys and
mislaid gloves,
a Christmas card with
two turtle doves,
red underpants
decidedly manky,
a barely used
lace-edged hanky,
a love letter
from David Pratt
to his girlfriend Sally,

what about that!
And right at the bottom
what I'm looking for,
the sports shirt I borrowed
from the boy next door . . .

Perhaps he won't bash me
now I've found it!

A Sea Creature Ate Our Teacher

Our teacher said it's always good
To have an inquisitive mind,
Then he told us, 'Go check the rock pools,
Let's see what the tide left behind.'

The muscles on his arms were bulging
As he pushed rocks out of the way.
'Identify what you see,' he called,
'Note it down in your books straight away.'

It was just as he spoke that we smelt it –
A stench like something rotten,
A wobbling mass of wet black skin
Like something time had forgotten.

In front of us snaking up from the pool
Was a hideous slime-soaked creature
With a huge black hole of a mouth
That vacuumed up our teacher.

I didn't actually see him go,
I was looking away at the time,
But I saw two legs sticking out
And trainers covered in slime.

But our teacher must have given this creature
Such chronic indigestion,
It found out that to try and digest him
Was simply out of the question.

It gave an almighty lunge of its neck
And spat our teacher out.
He was spread with the most revolting goo
And staggering about.

None of us moved to help him
As he wiped the gunge from his head.
We looked at each other and smirked,
'That'll teach *him* a lesson,' we said!

The I-Spy Book of Teachers

One point if you catch your teacher yawning.
Double that to two if later on you find her
snoring.
Three points if you hear your teacher singing
and four if it's a pop song not a hymn.
A generous five points if you ever see them
jogging
and six if you should chance upon them
snogging.
Seven if you ever find her on her knees and
praying
for relief from noisy boys who trouble her.
Eight if you should catch her buying underwear
and nine if she's seen jiving at a party.
And ten if you hear her say what a lovely class
she's got
for then you'll know there's something quite
seriously wrong with her.

The Mystery Walk

Tomorrow, Year 6, as part
of your week of activities,
we're going to take you all
on a mystery walk.

Where are we going, sir?

Well, it wouldn't be a mystery
if I told you, Barry, would it?

*But my mum likes to know
where I am, sir.*

Actually I don't know either,
I'm as much in the dark as you are.

*Oh come on, sir, you planned it,
you must know.*

Correction, Barry, Mr Winters planned it.

*Oh well, in that case it will be a mystery.
He can't even find his way to the right classroom
and he's been here twenty years . . .*

As I was saying, or trying to say,
you will all assemble here tomorrow
at nine o'clock.

What if it rains, sir?

You'll get wet, Barry,
W E T, wet.

But my mum doesn't like me getting wet, sir,
I catch cold easily,
I'll be off school . . .

Well, let us all hope for rai . . . a fine day,
all right, Barry, may I continue?

Oh yes, sir, please do, sir.

Make sure, Year 6, that you bring
a packed lunch . . .

Salami sandwiches. I love salami sandwiches,
don't you, sir?
Salami sandwiches with mustard, or pickle,
pickle's nice, sir . . .

I DON'T CARE WHAT YOU BRING, BARRY.
YOU CAN BRING A WHOLE STRING OF
SALAMI SAUSAGES,
HALF A DOZEN WATERMELONS,
A HUNDRED ICED BUNS
AND TEN GALLONS OF FIZZY DRINK,
THEN STUFF YOURSELF SILLY . . .
NOW JUST BE QUIET AND LET ME CONTINUE.

When the coach drops you off
you'll be given an envelope
with instructions for finding your way home.

What if we don't get home before dark, sir?
My mum . . .

I know, Barry, she doesn't like you being out
after dark.

That's right, sir.

Don't worry, Barry, we'll find you long before
dark.

So you do know where we're going, sir.
I knew it, he does know where we're going,
you can't trust teachers,
they say one thing and mean another.

Have you quite finished, Barry?

Yes, sir.

Right, take a walk, Barry.

Now, sir?

Right now, Barry. And, Barry . . .

Yes, sir.

This time I do know where you're going.

Where's that, sir?

To the head teacher, Barry, I've had enough.

But, sir . . . my mum doesn't like me going to the head teacher!!!

Jason, Who Got His Head Stuck

Jason, who got his head stuck between railings
in the Underground Works
on a trip to Dover Castle,
was merely demonstrating
how invaders could be repelled.
It was easy, he said,
all you had to do was to slip between the bars.
But they must have been thinner
in days of old – trimmer of figure.
And although he was pushed and pulled and
yanked,
Jason's head was firmly wedged.
'Step up on this ledge,' someone said,
'let's lower the angle, dangle him down.
Perhaps we can tip him head over heels,'
but two loud squeals from Jason
proved we were wrong.
He was captured tight between two posts
and what hurt most wasn't physical pain,
it was everyone standing jeering and laughing,
calling him daft to get himself trapped.

The safety officer wasn't happy,
he'd used up all his patience today
on silly children who thought
they could play the invading army,
climbing the banks, barmy they were,
and now this. 'Stand aside, I'll fix it,'
he said, but nothing he could do
would budge Jason's head.
'Call the fire brigade,' someone said.
So two burly fireman levered apart
the railings where Jason had stuck.
'Next time,' his teacher said, as Jason
withdrew his head. 'Next time,
we'll leave you there, like a criminal
in your pillory.' And Jason looked suitably
subdued till a TV crew popped up
from nowhere, to give him a moment
of glory on the regional news that night.

The Ghoul-School Bus

The ghoul-school bus
is picking up its cargo
of little horrors.

They must all be home
before first light, when today
turns into tomorrow.

All the sons and daughters of vampires,
little Igors and junior Fangs,
the teenage ghouls with their ghoulfriends
all wail as the bus bell clangs.

And the driver doesn't look well,
he's robed completely in black,
and the signboard says – Transylvania,
by way of hell and back.

The seats are slimy and wet,
there's a terrible graveyard smell,
all the small ghouls cackle and spit
and practise their ghoulish spells.

The witches are reading their ABCs,
cackling over 'D' for disease,
while tomboy zombies are falling apart
and werewolves are checking for fleas.

When the bus slows down to drop them off
at Coffin Corner or Cemetery Gates,
their mummies are waiting to greet them
with eyes full of anguish and hate.

The ghoul-school bus
is dropping off its cargo
of little horrors.

They must all be home
before first light, when today
turns into tomorrow.

GHOUL BUS

Who Did It?

'Who drew tattoos on the cavemen,
just who has been misbehaving?
And who stuck plasters on Guy Fawkes
so he looked like he'd cut himself shaving?

And who on earth added nose rings
to Henry the Eighth and his wives,
who's being so disrespectful
to all these historical lives?

And who tucked a mobile phone
under Florence Nightingale's chin?
Who dared to be so impolite
to our national heroine?

Who added rocket boosters
to a Roman chariot race?
And who pencilled in a moustache
on Queen Victoria's face?

Somebody better own up,
we'll be staying here till they do.'
Then our teacher looked straight at me,
'I bet I'm right – it was **YOU**!'

The School Goalie's Reasons

. . . why each goal shouldn't have been a goal in the match that ended 14–0 to the visiting team

1. It wasn't fair. I wasn't ready . . .
2. Their striker was offside. It was obvious . . .
3. Phil got in my way, he always gets in my way,
   he should be dropped . . .
4. I had something in my eye . . .
5. I hadn't recovered from the last one that went in,
   or the one before that . . .
6. I thought I heard our head teacher calling my name . . .
7. Somebody exploded a blown-up crisp bag behind me . . .
8. There was a beetle on the pitch, I didn't want
   to tread on it . . .
9. Somebody exploded another blown-up crisp bag behind me . . .
10. That girl in Year 5 was smiling at me.
    I don't like her doing that . . .
11. The goalposts must have been shifted, they weren't as wide
    as that before . . .

12. I thought I saw a UFO fly over the school . . .
13. There was a dead ringer for Gareth Bale watching us,
    he was spooky . . .

And goal number 14?
It just wasn't a goal, I'm sorry, it just wasn't a goal
and that's that . . .
OK?

Staff v Pupils

We felt like the cow that jumped over the moon,
we found ourselves dancing to some crazy tune
and although it was winter it felt like June,
the day we beat the teachers at football.

The staff really had very little support,
except, of course, for little Miss Short,
sixty years old, or so they say,
full of enthusiasm, wanted to play.

And the action ranged up and down the field,
no one giving way, no one ready to yield
the ball to allow the opponents to score,
this wasn't just football, it was out and out war.

There was nothing for it but to start playing
dirty,
so we did and our Head got really shirty
when somebody elbowed him in the face
as he started on yet another race
down the pitch with the ball at his feet
and we had to admit that his playing was neat.

Then we got the ball and were on a roll
straight down the pitch and heading for goal
till with one magnificently powerful shot
from Callum, that seemed to find the spot,
we were one–nil up, we were on our way
to victory, and a glorious day.

But that's when it happened, Mrs Dale got
knocked out,
Philip kicked the ball and then gave a shout,
but his teacher's reactions were far too slow,
the ball hit her head and then she didn't know
anything else until she came round
a hundred feet above the ground
in an air ambulance that jetted her off
to hospital where, still feeling rough,
they found there was nothing wrong with her
head,
although some of the younger kids swore she
was dead!

Then our Head said we should abandon it there,
it was only fair that he should declare
that the game had been void, no one had won,
after all it had only barely begun.
But we all though his decision was bad,
Callum had scored and it made us mad . . .

So cheated of probable victory
we decided to be contradictory
and declare ourselves winners nevertheless,
in our team's history a great success.

We felt like the cow that jumped over the moon,
we found ourselves dancing to some crazy tune,
and although it was winter it felt like June,
the day we beat the teachers at football.

TEACHERS ONLY
NO RIFF -RAFF

It Always Rains on Sports Day

It always rains on sports day,
or it has for weeks previously
and we're sitting there on coats
while the grass is steaming.
They might do better to issue us
with floats to cope with the dozens of puddles
that punctuate our running track.
And the winner might just as well swim home,
where his winner's rosette will be pinned
to a soggy vest.

It's always fun on sports day,
seeing who gets wettest.
You can bet your life
it won't be the teachers,
they come prepared and swan around
beneath their golf umbrellas,
while everyone else is perched on chairs
sinking deeper into the mud.

I hate sports day at our school:
you're out there trying to look cool
in front of parents, brothers, sisters,
grans, grandads, aunts, uncles, cousins,
the lady from two doors down
and your girlfriend from 3C.

And then you slam down in the mud
and you look like a player
in some rugby squad
rather than the bronzed, heroic Greek athlete
that you wanted them to see.

It always rains on sports day,
or it has for weeks previously.

This year it rained so much
that sports day was cancelled.

What a shame!

The Incredible Mrs Hulk

She laughs with us, she jokes with us,
she acts just like a big sister,
she's incredible, our teacher,
but we'd really like to meet Mister.

Often she says he's taken her
for a weekend together in Rome
or Paris maybe, or Amsterdam,
he's hardly ever home.

If only he could coach our team
for football on Saturday morning,
but he's out there somewhere saving us all
from some end-of-the-world-type warning.

But does he do anything ordinary?
We'd really like to know.
Is there some off-limits supermarket
where only superheroes go?

So we pester our Mrs Hulk
for her husband's autograph,
a message perhaps to inspire us
or maybe a photograph.

But he's always talking with presidents,
prime ministers, queens and kings.
He's far too busy she says
to think of such ordinary things.

So we just have to be patient
and pretend it's enough to know
that the teacher teaching us tables
is the wife of a superhero.

And although we know she's incredible
and she acts just like a big sister,
everyone in our class
is still desperate to meet Mister!

Sheep Wars: The Drama Teacher's Dilemma!

'We need more lines for Sheep 2 to say,
he doesn't say enough in our Nativity play.
His parents will complain if Sheep 2 is too dumb,
if they think his importance is less than Sheep 1.
They're the sort of parents who will time how
long
Sheep 2 is on stage compared with Sheep 1,
and whether he's centre stage or sidelined,
then demand his position be redefined.

So someone please write more lines, and fast,
if Sheep 2's appearance on stage is to last
as long as Sheep 1 and then that will avoid
any trouble from his parents if they are annoyed.
The last thing we want is Sheep Wars to break
out,
for the Sheepy parents to scream and shout.
This is, after all, the season of goodwill,
so fill Sheep 2's mouth, let him speak until
the curtain comes down on our school play
and his parents, happy, lead him away.'

The Crowd Scene

They say I can't act,
they say I can't dance.
They say I can't sing
but teacher won't give me a chance.

So I'm in the crowd scene again.

I asked to be a shepherd,
I begged to be a king.
I said that I'd play any part,
any person, any thing!

But I'm in the crowd scene again.

I wanted to be an angel
but all Mum's sheets were blue.
I even asked to be Joseph
but Mary said, 'Ugh, not you . . .'

So I'm in the crowd scene again.

I open and close my mouth,
teacher told me not to sing.
I move from place to place
and I watch and learn everything.

So if ever someone is absent,
I'll know it all by heart.
That's when I'll step from the crowd scene
to play my proper part.

The Wrong Words

We like to sing the wrong words
to Christmas Carols . . .

We three kings of Orient are,
One in a taxi, one in a car . . .

It drives our music teacher barmy,
his face turns red as a holly berry,
his forehead creases,
his eyes bulge.
It looks as if the top of his head
is about to lift like a saucepan lid
as he boils over . . .

His anger spills out
in an almighty shout . . .

'NO!' he roars . . .

'If you do that once more
I'll give you the kind of Christmas gift
you won't forget in a hurry . . .'

So we sing . . .
. . . *most highly flavoured lady* . . .

'IT'S FAVOURED,' he screams,
'NOT FLAVOURED . . .
What do you think she is,
an ice-cream cone?'

Then to cap it all
and drive him really wild
we sing of the shepherds
washing their socks,
till he slams down the piano lid
and takes off like a rocket
into the stratosphere,
lighting up the sky
like a Christmas star.

Windy Playground

They played blow-me-down in the yard,
letting the wind bully them,
coats above heads, arms spread wide,
daring the wind to do its worst.
They leaned forward against the blow
as it rallied and flung them back,
then coats puffed out like clouds
they returned to attack the blast,
while the gale drew a breath and then
pressed relentless. Till wild in defeat
and magnificent, they grouped again
and stretched their wings, stubborn
as early airmen.

Shoot the Messenger!

On playground duty, while sipping her tea,
Miss Martin told us stories.

'Long ago,' she said, 'if he brought bad news,
they used to shoot the messenger.

'This bringer of bad tidings,
message hidden, horse hard-ridden,
would burst upon the scene
with news of some huge defeat
in battle.

'And the first response would be,
pretend it hadn't happened,
make out they hadn't heard,
shoot the messenger,
forget his words.'

We listened, open-mouthed.
Miss Martin was smart,
her story must be true.

'Now,' she said, 'I've a job for someone.'

'Who wants to go to the staffroom
to tell the teachers
it's end of break?'

STAFF ROOM
BREAK'S OVER
DON'T HIT ME!

The Puddle in Our Playground

It seems as if it's rained for weeks
and a deep puddle covers our playground.

There's something not quite right about it,
something frightening, no doubt about it.
But everyone's out there moving round it
till our caretaker says, 'Come on, get out of it,
I'll brush this clear in no time.'

But a wave rolls over the debris and muck,
the puddle gives a slurp and a suck
and his broom just disappears!

'There's something queer about that puddle,
steer clear of it,' our caretaker says.

But Gavin drops his boot in, and Alison her
 lunch.
Well, here's a hunch, whatever's unwanted
throw it into the puddle.

Balls, homework, coats all disappear,
'Hey, let's show teacher – bring her near,
perhaps we can give her one big push . . .'

Now where's the headmaster,
fetch him quick . . .

We've got our own Bermuda Triangle,
phone the papers, phone the TV,
it's not every day you see
something like this . . .

Maybe if it rains and rains
and rains and rains and rains
this puddle will swallow our school,
that'll really be cool!

The Worry Box

I'm worried about the worry box
in our classroom.

Our teacher
(who's really awfully nice)
said that we had to write
down our worries
on pieces of paper
and drop them into
the worry box.

But I'm worried
I don't have any worries
and I've never disobeyed
my teacher before.

So I'm worried about the worry box
in our classroom.

Should I make up some worries?
(I'm good at making things up,
my teacher says.)
I could say that I'm bullied,
or my mum keeps shouting at me,
or my dog's run away.

That worry box is worrying me.
I've never felt
quite so worried before
and maybe if my teacher knows
how much it worries me
she'll take it away.

So I've written down my worry
on a piece of paper
and dropped it into
the worry box –

'I'm worried about the worry box
in our classroom.'

High-Flyers

We thought our teacher was ordinary,
we thought she was really boring,
she always looked tired from teaching us
and at weekends was probably snoring.
We thought she led a quiet life
at home, feet up, being lazy,
but it seemed that our teacher had always
  wanted
to try something really crazy . . .

She told us all in the middle of maths
she'd be doing a bungee jump,
and we were appalled, we could see her
hitting the ground with a mighty thump.
We were worried it wouldn't be anything else
but one hundred per cent disaster,
our teacher laid out in a hospital bed
with both of her legs in plaster.

She'd be raising lots of money, she said,
for her favourite charity,
but we felt it would all be far too much
for a woman of fifty-three.
Then she said, I hope you'll support me,
I expect you all to be there.
It's Saturday afternoon at three,
halfway through our village fair.

So we all turned up and had to admit
our teacher looked fantastic,
and we watched amazed as she bounced around
on the end of a length of elastic.
She was kitted out in a jumpsuit
that was zigzag yellow and black
and reminded us all of an angry wasp
that was moving in to attack.

But that wasn't the only surprise of the day
because tumbling down from the sky
was a team of freefall divers
who we couldn't identify,
till their parachutes suddenly blossomed
and somebody started to laugh,
when drifting gently down to earth
came the rest of our school staff!

The Theme for This Week Is 'Laziness'

(From a sign in the hall at Godshill School, Isle of Wight!)

I've never been very good at school,
it's not often that I do well,
but the theme for this week is 'laziness'
and that's something at which I excel.

I have no trouble being lazy,
it's really no effort at all.
I prefer to watch television
than be outside chasing a ball.

I'm always last to finish my work,
I always come last in a race.
I never get any group points,
my teacher says I'm a disgrace.

But everyone's good at something
and at laziness I'll be the best.
I know that I'm good at laziness
and I'll happily take any test.

Perhaps next week we'll do 'carelessness',
there's 'clumsiness' and 'thoughtlessness' too.
I'm good at all these but I'm just no good
at subjects they want me to do.

I'm a lazy good-for-nothing,
that's something I've always been told,
but if laziness were an Olympic sport
then I know I'd be going for gold!

What Teachers Wear in Bed

(After overhearing a conversation between six teachers in the staffroom at ______ School. Shh! Better not say which one – it could be yours . . . !)

It's anybody's guess
what teachers wear in bed at night,
so we held a competition
to see if any of us were right.

We did a spot of research,
although some of them wouldn't say,
but it's probably something funny
as they look pretty strange by day.

Our head teacher's quite old fashioned,
he wears a Victorian nightshirt,
our sports teacher wears her tracksuit
and sometimes her netball skirt.

That new teacher in the infants
wears bedsocks with see-through pyjamas,
our deputy head wears a T-shirt
he brought back from the Bahamas.

We asked our secretary what she wore
but she shooed us out of her room,
and our teacher said her favourite nightie
and a splash of expensive perfume.

And Madamoiselle, who teaches French,
is really very rude,
she whispered, 'Alors! Don't tell a soul,
but I sleep in the . . . back bedroom!'

Mr Frost

Looking in Mr Frost's eyes
is like being lost
in icy wastes.
He's Antarctica
all the year round.
He's permafrost,
frozen ground.

Miss Honey

When we first discovered Miss Honey
was to be our new Year 6 teacher,
we gaped, mouths open, stopped in our tracks
at the sight of this heaven-sent creature.

She was trim, she was neat, she was lovely,
and less than a hundred years old.
She was every fairy-tale princess
with a smile like liquid gold.

Most of the boys lost their hearts
and would have died for her then and there,
captivated by the pull of her eyes
and the way she flicked back her hair.

They were hooked from the very first moment
she asked them to do her a favour,
they were Knights of King Arthur's Round Table
with courage that would never waver.

She wafted between the tables
like a model more used to the catwalk,
while her voice was like honey itself
and we'd much rather listen than talk.

She was wonderful, she was gorgeous,
she was Beauty and we'd been such beasts,
but Miss Honey tamed the wildest class
and all resistance ceased.

Our Teacher

Our teacher taps his toes,
keeping the beat to some silent tune
only he knows.

Our teacher drums his fingers,
on his desk, on the window,
on anything, when the room is quiet,
when we're meant to be writing
in silence.

Our teacher cracks his knuckles,
clicks his fingers, grinds his teeth,
his knees are knocking the edge of his desk,
he breathes to a rhythmical beat.

When he turns his head in a certain way
there's a bone that cracks in his neck.
When he sinks to the floor
we often think he'll stay on his knees
for ever more, he's such a physical wreck!

Our teacher bangs his head against the wall
(or pretends to) when Wendy comes up
with another dumb remark.

Our teacher says we annoy him
with all our silly fuss.
Perhaps he's never really thought
how much he irritates us.

GRIND!
CRACK!
CLICKETY! CLACKETY! CLICK! CLACK! CLICK!
DRUM! DIDDLY -DUM!
THUMPITY! TUMPITY! WHUMP!
TIPPITY! TAPPITY! TIP! TAP! TIP!

Escape Route

When our teacher came to school today
he looked bright and happy, not old and grey,
not the usual bear whose head was sore,
and we hadn't seen him like this before.
He parked his car in our head-teacher's space,
you should have seen the look on her face
as she swept like a hurricane into our room,
and it brightened up our Monday gloom.
But instead of looking a picture of worry
or smiling nervously and saying sorry
he'd go out and shift it straight away,
our teacher told her that from today
she could stay and teach his class,
and the look on her face was like frosted glass.
He ripped up test papers in front of her eyes,
then jumped up and down, and to our surprise
planted a slobbery kiss on her cheek,
and just for a moment she couldn't speak
till he told us how on Saturday night
his lottery numbers had all been right.
Then a noise from outside made us all look
  round
as a helicopter landed in our school grounds,
and our teacher said, 'It's my taxi at last,
this school, all of you, are now in my past.'
Then while we watched, the big blades whirred
and he left for the sky as free as a bird.

And his car is still parked in our head-teacher's space.
You should have seen the look on her face!

Romance

I know there's something going on
between Mr Phipps and Miss White.
I've seen them in the car park,
how they linger when they say goodnight.

I caught them once in the TV room
with all the blinds drawn down.
He said that he'd lost his glasses,
I bet they were fooling around.

When she wafts into our classroom
and catches him by surprise,
nothing is too much trouble,
there's a faraway look in his eyes.

Quite what she sees in him
none of us really knows:
She's quite fashion conscious,
he wears some terrible clothes.

We think he sends her notes:
please tick if you really love me,
and if she's slow to reply
we've seen him get awfully angry.

But when they're lovey-dovey,
he's just like a little boy,
cracking jokes and smiling again,
filling our class with his joy.

Truants

Mr Flint drove to school each day
with Mrs Price,
along the way they shared conversation,
shared their troubles, shared petrol money,
and then one day,
one warm bright day at the start of summer,
when the last thing they felt like doing
was teaching troublesome children,
they drove on,
right past the school gates.
Several children saw them,
several children waved
but they took no notice.
They drove on through towns and villages,
past cows and horses at rest on hillsides,
past a windmill, its sails turning lazily,
until finally they could travel no more
and ahead of them stretched the sea.
Then they turned and looked at each other
and wondered what they'd done,
but as they'd driven such a long way,
they thought they might as well enjoy
themselves.

So they paddled in the sea,
they skipped and chased along the beach,
they flipped stones into the water,
they built a magnificent sandcastle.
For lunch they ate ice cream and candyfloss.
Then they rode a miniature train
to the end of the pier and back,
played a double round of crazy golf,
lost lots of money in amusement arcades
and shared two bags of fish and chips
with a gang of gulls on the prom.

They drove home in silence,
past the horses and cows
and the windmill, now still,
past the school gates,
now firmly locked for the night.

And when they sneaked back to school next day,
all sheepish and shy,
embarrassed at the fuss they'd caused,
their head teacher
made them go outside at playtime
for a whole week.

Teachers' Awards

At the end of each summer term,
amid much hugging and hilarity,
school teachers congratulate each other
on surviving yet another school year.

So let's hear it for Mrs King,
our queen of the big production number,
always on a short fuse,
especially on duty days.

And not forgetting Mr White,
for staying calm when the classroom radiator
leaked rusty water all over
his recently completed pile of report cards.

Let's hear it for Mrs Salmon,
who restrained herself quite admirably
when the class gerbil
ate her winning lottery ticket.

And for Mr Middleton, who has eaten school
  dinners
for each day of his twenty-year career,
unable to be with us tonight,
but we hope he'll be out of hospital soon.

And the romance-of-the-year award
goes to Miss Buchanan and Mr Duke,
they're dreadfully drippy when they're together,
it really makes us . . . feel unwell!

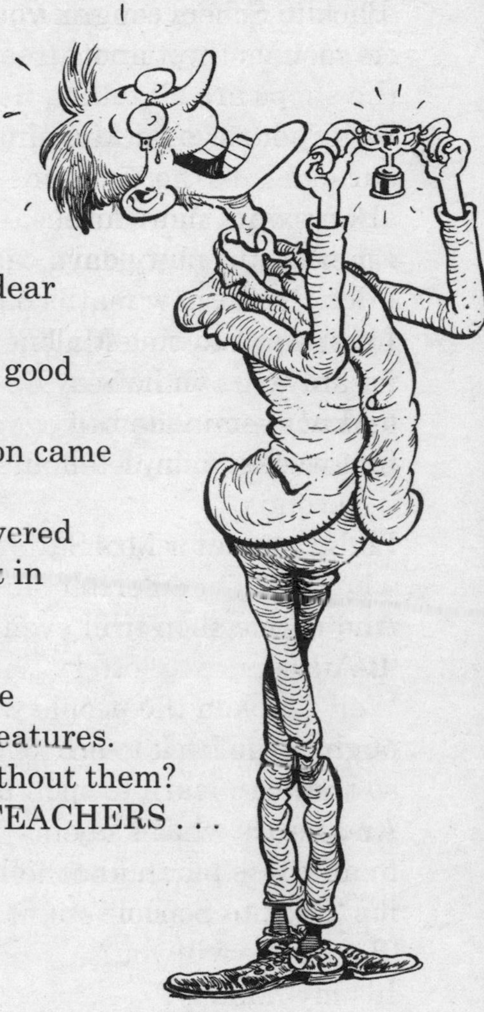

And last of all for our dear
head teacher,
who led us all through good
times and bad,
till our school inspection came
along
and he suddenly discovered
a pressing engagement in
Barbados.

So let's hear it for those
fabulous, wonderful creatures.
Where would we be without them?
Let's hear it for THE TEACHERS . . .

Back to School

A week after the holiday begins
and there it is, in every shop window in town,
'Back to School' – I ask you.
As soon as they set us free,
the shops are all telling us
we've got to go back again.

I don't want new clothes,
I don't want new pencil cases,
I don't want new maths equipment,
I just want to be left alone,
I want to be on holiday
and not reminded how
in 4 weeks, 5 days, 7 hours, 39 minutes and 13
  seconds
I'll be back at school.

And in one shop they even spelled it
'B-A-K'.
Well I reckon the people who wrote that sign
ought to go back to school too,
so they can learn to spell properly.
And here's what I say
to all those places that tell me
it's 'Back to School' –
'Back off – will you?
It's my holiday!'

BAK TO SKOOL!
ANY DAY NOW!
SCHOOL

In this fantastic collection of poems Brian Moses tells us about cats, dogs, dragons, New York, space, dinosaurs, spider-swallowing, why he has given up playing air guitar, why you cannot take a lobster through security, the ghosts of London Underground and why fairies must have taken his brother!

What Are We Fighting For?

Brian Moses and Roger Stevens

Fascinating and moving in equal measure, this brand-new collection of poetry from Brian Moses and Roger Stevens explores the topic of war in a brilliantly accessible way for younger readers.

Find out about incredibly brave animals on the battlefield, the day soldiers played football in no-man's-land, poems about rationing and what it was like to be an evacuee, plus poems about the idea of warfare, asking the question What Are We Fighting For?

NEW POEMS ABOUT WAR

AUTHOR NEWS · BONUS CONTENT
VIDEOS · GAMES · PRIZES . . .
AND MORE!